COMMUNICATING WITH EMPATHY

Understanding and applying empathy personally and professionally

Ifra Publication

CONTENTS

Title Page

Copyright

What you'll learn 1

About 2

Who this Book is for 3

Introduction 4

Understanding Personalities 5

Working with Others 6

Communicating with Others 8

Persuading Others 10

Personalities Matter 12

Preferences and Tendencies 15

Leading With 17

Wisdom from a Retired Therapist 19

Generalisations and Assumptions 23

Gaming Assessments 25

Moods and Circumstances 27

Critics of Assessments 28

Assessments Are Not Tests 30

Allowing Change Over Time 31

Quick Recap 34

Understanding the MBTI   35

A Key to MBTI Results: Root Questions   36

Simplifying Types of Descriptions   42

Understanding ISTJ (Inspector)   44

Understanding ISFJ (Protector)   46

Understanding ESFJ (Provider)   48

Understanding INFJ (Counsellor)   50

Forgiveness, Flexibility, and Job Fit   52

What This Means   54

Quick Recap   56

Understanding DiSC   57

DiSC Overview   59

Observable Behaviours   61

Debrief Behaviours   63

Complementary People   65

Complementary Styles   67

Behavioural Strengths and Soft Skills   69

Assessment Results and Your Brand   72

Quick Recap   75

Better Relationships and Communication   76

Understanding Yourself   77

Understanding Others   79

Allowing for Flexibility and Scalability   81

Best Roles for Personalities   83

Two Keys to Your Success   85

Personalities and Working with Others   87

Personalities and Communication with Others   89

Personalities and Influencing Others   91

Your Lifelong Journey   93

Conclusion   95

WHAT YOU'LL LEARN

1. Understanding what it is and how it works
2. The different types of empathy and when to use them
3. Empathetic listening
4. How to make some space and develop self awareness
5. Master how to have conversations with difficult people while keeping your cool
6. Give effective feedback that people can hear without defensiveness
7. Ask for the feedback you need to do your job more successfully
8. Present your ideas more persuasively
9. Think on your feet in any situation

ABOUT

Our professional connections are far too frequently more difficult than necessary. This has an effect on productivity, morale, and job satisfaction. You will learn the fundamentals of personality differences in this Book, Communicating with Empathy, which will enable you to work and interact with others more effectively.

You will first learn about the fundamentals of personality as well as tests that aid in intercultural communication. The Myers-Briggs and DiSC tests will next be discussed, along with how to interpret test results. Finally, you'll discover how to put all of this knowledge together to enhance your communication and working relationships.

After completing this Book, you will have the people skills and personality understanding required to flourish in your work by engaging with others more successfully.

WHO THIS BOOK IS FOR

1. Busy professionals who need to improve their presentation and communication skills quickly -- and who don't have time for an in-person workshop
2. People managers at all levels who need to give more effective performance feedback - and model how to receive feedback well
3. Anyone who has to present ideas to internal or external audiences
4. Those who struggle with conflict and tricky conversations with colleagues, customers, clients, and others
5. People in any industry who want to be seen as more confident, credible, and compelling communicators

INTRODUCTION

Hey everyone. My name is Ifra, and welcome to my Book, Communicating with Empathy. In this Book, we're going to talk about our relationships with people who we work with. I created this Book because people are different and working with different personalities can be confusing. Some of the major topics we'll cover include personalities in general and what learning about personalities means, the Myers-Briggs personality assessment, as well as the DiSC personality assessment.

We'll talk about how knowledge about personalities can improve our relationships and help us become better communicators. By the end of this Book, you should have a much better idea of how you can work with people who have different personalities. From here, you should feel comfortable diving into Communicating with Empathy with Books on becoming a better listener, how to get your next promotion, and leading with emotional intelligence.

I hope you'll join me on this journey to learn more about yourself and others with the Communicating with Empathy Book, at Amazon.

UNDERSTANDING PERSONALITIES

I n this chapter, I'll lay a foundation for the rest of the Book. It's important we have enough context around the ideas of personalities and how people work and communicate so we can understand how we work and communicate. Digging into some of the tools without this foundation or without proper context could set you up to misunderstand or even misuse information you collect about yourself or others.

Tools such as personality assessments can help you better understand yourself and others, perhaps enriching relationships and being in a better position to help others. I imagine you've had confusing work relationships. I've been confused by some of the people I've worked with over the years. Maybe they said something weird or made decisions that just didn't make sense. I've learned that many times they weren't out to be harmful or malicious, rather they were doing what they thought was best for the organisation and maybe even for me.

Understanding their personalities was key for me to have the proper perspective for what was happening around me. This Book is about learning about others, as well as yourself. Let's get started.

WORKING WITH OTHERS

There are few roles where you don't have to work with others. Even the most introverted person has to interface with others sometimes. Normally, we have a boss and colleagues we have to work with, sometimes we have prospects and clients to take care of. For some of us, this is fine and even exciting. I've found I can't go long without interacting with others, even though I consider myself introverted.

When the COVID pandemic impacted our workforce in 2020 and people were working remotely alone, there was a lot of conversation about how working in isolation impacted our productivity, our mental health, the future of work, and more. For others, working with others feels annoying or maybe some level of terrifying. I've known people who are excellent at what they do, but I'm not sure I've heard them say 10 sentences over the years. They take pride in their work and the quality they deliver, but they don't want to interact with others to the point of actively avoiding interaction.

Understanding our own personalities and tendencies is important. When we understand how and when we want to interact with others, we can strategize how to best work with them. We might realise when our best time to work with others is or how we best communicate, educate, and influence.

Understanding others can help you figure out and accept why, how, and when they interact with and work with you. Things we assume about those we work with can be entirely wrong, especially when we don't understand ourselves or them.

COMMUNICATING
WITH OTHERS

I'm fascinated by excellent communicators. You have people who can get in front of an audience and command a room with people on the edge of their seats and anxious to hear more. You have great leaders who seem to fill a room with their enthusiasm and positive energy, and you have those who are much less visible, quieter, and seem to be more reserved, but even those people can be excellent communicators.

Communication comes natural to some, but others, like me, need to continually work at it. I should mention, there are a number of Books on Amazon that help you improve your communication skills. Check my profile after you read this online Book and you'll find some. At the core of effective communication is knowing your message and what you want people to walk away with. That might be information or motivation to act on something. Another critical element of communication is understanding how you tend to communicate.

Perhaps you have a tendency to be overbearing, very direct or use subtle hints. Your communication is probably influenced by your culture. It is definitely influenced by your personality. People who are results-driven are more likely to get right to the point and not consider feelings than people who are driven by relationships.

Understanding yourself is critical; understanding who you communicate with is essential. You may be results driven, but if the people around you are more relationship driven, they will get tired of your impersonal, straight-to-the-point communication.

I'm not saying you have to change how you communicate. That's a decision you'll have to make based on multiple factors. What I'm saying is that when you understand your communication tendencies and the tendencies of those you communicate with and to, you can be a more effective communicator. I'm not sure there are many more important skills to give you better results or relationships than really effective communication.

I hope as you progress through this Book, you come to understand how you can more effectively communicate to the different types of people you interact with.

PERSUADING OTHERS

Years ago I was listening to a presentation by one of my business mentors. He said he has two main things he wants to accomplish when he presents. Those are to impact and to inspire. I thought that was really profound. It made me think about why I communicate with anyone. Whether I'm talking to one person or hundreds of people, I too want to impact and inspire. When we impact and inspire others, we're in a great position to persuade and influence.

Learning how to persuade and influence others can be a superpower. Seriously, one of the most powerful skills you can learn. I have friends who are masters of persuasion. Watching them communicate with others is fascinating. This superpower could be abused, and by no means am I asking you to think about how to persuade someone in an abusive or malicious way, but I am asking you to think about how you can be more effective in your communication and become more persuasive in your arguments. Of course, persuading others doesn't mean you always need or want to have your way, but as you seek to understand and seek truth, you can persuade others to seek to understand and seek truth.

Use these new powers of persuasion and influence for good and see what that does to your team and productivity. Practise persuading others to come to your way of thinking or get bought into your proposals. As you learn more about yourself, your personality, and tendencies to communicate and learn more about others and their tendencies to receive information, you'll be on a path to more effectively persuade others

PERSONALITIES MATTER

I want to share a few experiences I've had when working with others who have personalities I just didn't understand. While there was plenty of frustration, we generally got our work done. I think there's a balance between I always like everyone I work with all the time and we are a highly productive team. The purpose of work is not to always like everyone you work with all the time, but working with people we don't like or who don't like us could be miserable. You'll have to figure out where that line is for your own job satisfaction, but just realise it's not always going to be awesome.

Rusty, which is his real name, was one of my best bosses ever. Rusty is the kind of boss or colleague you would follow around as long as you could, even changing jobs and companies. Rusty is a phenomenal, outstanding human and leader. I was in a meeting with Rusty when he was giving me some direction on a project and I was suffering pretty harshly from imposter syndrome. I kept wondering, why did he even hire me? Why not just do this himself since he has thought through every last detail? I didn't realise two things. First, he was doing a massive brain dump with a lot of detail, but he wasn't expecting me to follow every direction or implement every detail.

He wanted to do a knowledge transfer and then free me so I could bring my best ideas and work to his ideas. Second, I didn't understand that my greatest value was to execute on his vision. I was wondering, why doesn't he do this instead of appreciating that he trusted me to be an extension of him, which is really quite flattering. Years ago, I worked as a web developer with Sally, which is not her real name. Sally was a frustrated person. She was fairly new to her role and didn't understand enough about technology to effectively manage me. She had a lot of personal things going on, which only complicated our relationship and communication.

Anyway, Sally was usually very short with me. After a while, I figured out she was not angry or impatient with me, rather she was frustrated with herself and her ability to manage me and my work. I felt uncomfortable around her because of the way she acted around me, but if I just understood her need for perfection, especially in her own role, I would have understood her issues had nothing to do with me and I would have thought and behaved differently. I worked with a colleague who was always very short with me. I honestly thought they hated me or despised working with me. I later learned through observation that this person was like this with everyone. They were very competent in their role, but left a lot of people not liking working with them.

When I realised that was just how they were and it wasn't anything personal or a reflection of who they liked, I changed how I worked with them. Honestly, this realisation into how they worked and communicated changed our relationship entirely. Even though they still act that way, I give them a lot of leeway. I've changed my expectations. Not only are we good together, but we found more opportunities to work together. I'm sure in your personal and professional life you have your own stories similar to these. How people act, communicate, and think impacts work relationships, productivity, and job satisfaction. Understanding ourselves and others can change everything.

It's like we see things through a different lens, a much clearer lens. Understanding personalities is critical when working with someone who seems lazy, when working with someone who solves problems different than you do, when working with customers who seem to not want to talk to you, when working with a boss who regularly rejects your ideas, when asking for a raise or presenting career changing information, when asking someone for help, when trying to persuade others. Understanding personalities, yours and those of others, can greatly impact your communication and effectiveness in these and other situations you encounter multiple times a day.

PREFERENCES AND TENDENCIES

I recently had a great chat with Jane Roqueplot, a friend who specialises in training leaders and coaches on using the DiSC assessment, which we'll go into deeper later. Jane has been teaching resume writers, career coaches, and HR and business managers how to use DiSC as a tool to help with various things, including how to position a job candidate better, jobs to focus on, as well as how teams can work better with one another.

The premise for working better as a team is that if you understand yourself and one another, you can understand how best to work and communicate with one another. As I was talking with Jane about this Book, she reemphasized something I had heard before. Results from the DiSC assessment, like the Myers-Briggs assessment, help you understand tendencies and preferences. Instead of declaring what your personality is, which can be too stereotyped, think of assessment results as a tool to help you understand how you prefer to give or receive information, make decisions, etc. Assessment results help you understand how you tend to act or react, think or talk, and accept or analyse information you get.

In turn, this impacts how you give information. This is a really profound concept. When I first learned about these assessments, which I wrongly thought were tests, I thought you would find out what your personality was and then you pretty much acted within the scope of the definition of that personality. It was as if your personality definition locked you into how you would be, react, think, and communicate for the rest of your life. This felt very confining. Instead of thinking of assessment results as absolutes, think about how they can help you understand tendencies.

You tend to want more data when making decisions, you tend to want to talk about personal and family things before jumping into business matters, you tend to want to get work done quickly and completely, you tend to value processes over people or people over processes. Understanding what people tend to do is empowering. Thinking about personalities through the lens of tendencies instead of discrete rules or boundaries changed the way I looked at these assessments.

LEADING WITH

Another really cool concept I picked up as I've studied this topic over the years is also empowering. Let's take a simple example and say that someone is really introverted. You would expect an introvert to not want to be around a lot of people, not want to talk to or present to large groups, not do well in a network environment, things like that. These are generalisations we make about introverts, right? What happens then when an introvert is in a network meeting and they seem like the life of the party. They're loud, converse well, and hold their own. If you didn't know they were introverts, you would think they were the most extroverted person around.

Well, first of all, introvert doesn't mean you don't like or can't be around people or that you can't have conversations with humans. The newer way I've heard introverts described is how they recharge. The introvert recharges by themselves, while the extrovert recharges by being around others. Instead of going into the definition of what an introvert is or isn't, I want to focus on a different idea, which is that we can have personality traits that are more dominant than others, but even the less dominant traits can come out sometimes.

My wife refers to this as leading with. You might usually lead with certain tendencies, but in different circumstances, perhaps influenced by moods or urgencies or whatever, your less dominant tendencies might come out and be more dominant. This is not an unexplainable phenomenon or even rare, it's just respecting ourselves and others and recognizing that we are dynamic, complex creatures who aren't always going to act in a certain way, regardless of what our assessment results are. Pay attention to what you and others lead with, but don't be shocked when you see communication or behaviour that contradicts what you expect.

WISDOM FROM A
RETIRED THERAPIST

There's a lot of controversy around defining personality traits, as well as assessments like the Myers-Briggs. I reached out to a friend, Vern Cox, who has had a long career in therapy. He's been a marriage and family therapist, as well as a psychotherapist.

My question to him was, is the Myers-Briggs a legitimate tool? His response was, "The Myers-Briggs Type Indicator is a legitimate tool, and I think it's one of the better ones." He continues, "The only thing I don't like about it, and most other assessments, is this: if you score only 1 point different in one of the categories, you're completely in that category, even though your score is very slightly in that category." He continues, "You are then boxed in rather than having a continuum that would indicate how different you are in each category."

This is the same criticism I've heard from others that Myers-Briggs and other personality assessments don't take into account how close you are to another category. By the way, there are 16 categories or results from a Myers-Briggs assessment. It might be nice if you could somehow say you were very close to another category. I took a quick and free Myers-Briggs assessment online. There are plenty of sites to choose from to do this. My results were ESFJ. One of the sites I used, 16personalities.com, gave me a beautiful graphic to help me understand how E or S or F or J I really am. As you can see in my results, I'm J for judging.

The graphic indicated I was really close to the alternative, P. I found that to be really interesting information. I could easily go either way. In contrast, it said I was a strong extrovert and not very close to being introverted. While not perfect, this gives me data points to think about. I want to see how close I am to other categories. Instead of just saying I'm an E, or extroverted, and hear all the characteristics, I want to know how much of an extrovert I am or how close I actually get to being introverted. Someone else recommended understanding the differences between each of the results. They said you can then do a self-assessment to perhaps get more accurate results than you might get by taking a questionnaire.

Whatever your assessment results are, you might not be that 100%. You can also change over time. I took four assessments within an hour and a half and I got different results from each one. This Book isn't about beating up or discounting any personality assessment. Instead, I want you to have a foundation to help you understand why people do things the way they do and how they make decisions.

I want you to work on improving relationships with others and be more effective with your persuasion skills, and I definitely want you to learn more about yourself and your tendencies and what you lead with

Sliding Scale vs. Absolute

Let's build on my therapist friend's problem he had with personality assessments, which was that they label you with clear definitions of who you are or how you'll act. Remember, he said he would like to see how close you are to other labels or groupings. Your tendencies might not fall squarely into one group or another, rather they might be a combination of various groups.

I like to think about our personalities as not so finite, like you would have with absolutes, but rather on something of a sliding scale. A sliding scale helps you know how close you are to different categories. This can give you a better idea of which characteristics you tend to gravitate towards. I like to think of your personality, tendencies, and preferences being on a sliding scale. An E on your Myers-Briggs doesn't mean you're completely extroverted. You might usually be extroverted, but sometimes tend to act like an introvert.

Thinking about the results of personality assessments along a sliding scale can help us avoid stereotyping people. Instead of making assumptions based on their results, we can think, I know you tend to be an extrovert, but that doesn't mean you'll act like an extrovert in every situation. Sometimes we think we can accurately predict how someone will act based on their personality results, but we wouldn't be right all the time. I'm at either end of the scale and can tend to be more extroverted or introverted, depending on multiple factors, like who is in the room, how comfortable I am with the subject matter or what mood I'm in, even how tired or hungry I might be.

When we think of results along a sliding scale instead of absolutes, it's easier to understand why someone did something that seems contrary to their assessment results. We, as humans, are complex beings. We're allowed to do things differently than what our personality assessment dictates. A few minutes ago we talked about preferences and tendencies. Those two words do not indicate absolutes. They actually leave a lot of room open for variances.

You prefer to do something a certain way, but that doesn't mean you always or even mostly do it that way. This is nicely aligned with the concept of a sliding scale. The sliding scale is an important concept when it comes to assessment results. It can help you come to terms with your own and others' categorizations.

GENERALISATIONS AND ASSUMPTIONS

One of the reasons people dislike personality assessments is they tend to put us into discrete buckets, I think to help us understand people easier. For example, if I say someone is introverted, you immediately have some idea of how they'll act. A problem with that is I might have some assumptions about how they'll act while you have other assumptions, and both of us could be wrong. Coming up with labels and categories to understand others can be convenient, but they can be misleading.

As we talked about with the sliding scale concept, labels could also be wrong. I've been in conversations where people say, for example, John is an introvert, so he won't want to meet with the executives to pitch our ideas. That could be a misuse or an abuse of these assessment results. Maybe John would love nothing more than to represent our team and make some very strong arguments to pitch our ideas. Maybe he's been taking Books to improve his presentation and persuasion skills.

Declaring labels and categories and then making judgments and decisions based on those labels and categories without having the proper conversations could have an impact on our productivity, careers, effectiveness, relationships, and more. I've seen great leaders move beyond the labels and assumptions and sit down with people to ask them what they think, where they're at, and if they'd be interested in new opportunities. When we skip those conversations and only use assumptions based on labels, we're missing out on a lot of great potential.

We tend to despise stereotyping, but that's what happens when we generalise and assume based on labels. And we all do it in many parts of our life. It's easy for us to do it, but when we're the victim of stereotyping, we tend to think, but I'm different, I really am. The funny thing is we even generalise and label ourselves, which can be harmful if left unchecked.

I find people tend to be harder on themselves or not appreciate the good as much as others can. My friend Vern, the therapist, said this, which is a way to think beyond assumptions. "I don't want just the four letters to tell me who and what I am. I want to understand how close I am to the other four letters.

GAMING
ASSESSMENTS

A nother issue I hear about with these assessments and have even had problems with myself is the tendency to game the assessment. This is tricky for me because I want to answer each question correctly, but sometimes that means I answer based on what I think the ideal answer is and not what my honest answer is. Gaming an assessment might mean we think about how someone we admire might answer a question or how we wish we would respond if we were better people or how we would answer if we had habits or thoughts that were better than what we have now.

I've been instructed to answer questions based on my gut feel instead of overanalyzing or thinking too much about a question and what the "right" answer is. When you read a question, your first reaction or thought is what you should go with. That's what I've been told when taking these assessments. I tend to overthink the question or my responses. I usually read a question and think, this question is worded so horribly. It can mean too many different things. How should I answer so I look better? This is not the way to answer the questions. When you read a question and know your response will make you not as professional, nice or productive as you want, it's easy to answer in a way that makes you look better.

At least that's what I find myself doing. Again, try not to think too deeply about your responses and answer honestly. There isn't a right or wrong answer or a right or wrong personality or label or categorization. The goal is to learn about yourself and help others understand you better. Gaming the assessment won't help you get to the truth you want and need. The more honest you are in your answers, the better your results should be. If your answers are ideal, but not reflective of who you are, your results won't be as meaningful.

MOODS AND CIRCUMSTANCES

Unfortunately, our mood and circumstances could impact how we answer, and thus the results. If I'm happy and optimistic, I might respond differently than if I were to have spent a few days being depressed and discouraged about my future. Current life situations could change how you respond to assessment questions. Imagine responding to questions a day after learning about the death of someone who was close to you. I can't even imagine those responses being the same as how you would respond on a routine day.

I read about someone whose normal result was an extrovert; however, this person lost their spouse and a few months later when they took the assessment, they scored as an introvert. If you take the assessment every month, I bet you would get different results every month. Sometimes the results would be nominally different, other times they could be significantly different.

What does this mean? To me, it means we can't have the results define us or anyone forever. Even if they seem to perfectly explain someone, people change, circumstances change. We need to allow people's personalities and tendencies to be more fluid rather than extremely well defined and constant.

CRITICS OF ASSESSMENTS

For any given personality assessment tool, you'll find plenty of critics. They can range from people who don't like assessments in general to people who love one tool or methodology and therefore don't like others. A quick online search of MBTI and critics will show things like misleading, inaccurate, unscientific, pretty much meaningless, hogwash, pseudoscience, and questionable. You can find articles with titles similar to MBTI, the Fad that Won't Die. No assessment is flawless.

Knowing they aren't perfect, we can still take the results and use them as data points. If we want to improve our teams, our communication, our productivity, and ourselves, let's take multiple data points from which we can make decisions. When I first created this Book, an article I read said there are about 2.5 million Myers-Briggs assessments taken each year. A few years later, a new article says 3.5 million assessments are taken each year. Other assessments, such as the DiSC assessment, have also grown in popularity. I'm not sure this is because people are dying to learn more about themselves.

I'm guessing this is getting pushed by HR departments and organisational leaders to better understand cultural fit, cultural differences to make hiring and promotion decisions, etc. Instead of focusing on the flaws, I want to focus on what we can learn from these assessment tools. I want to know how they can help us as we work with, communicate with, and persuade other people.

ASSESSMENTS
ARE NOT TESTS

I 've talked about this a bit, and perhaps you've caught on to it, but I don't call these tools personality tests. No one in the industry does. A test has right or wrong answers, and you can get a perfect score on a test. You can also fail a test. An assessment simply assesses where you are at, and there aren't right or wrong answers. Instead of the right answer, we want you to give the most accurate answer for you.

Your most accurate answer for a question could be polar opposite than my most accurate answer, but neither of us would be wrong, nor would either of us fail. Assessments are designed to give us a better diagnostic on our personality or our preferences and tendencies.

What this means is that you don't have to go into these assessments nervous or worried about any particular result. The results are simply there to help you understand yourself and others better. There is no right or wrong when it comes to personality assessment results, it's just you.

ALLOWING CHANGE OVER TIME

I've talked about this a little during this Book, but I want to be explicitly clear on an important concept. You must allow for change over time. Your results today could be different, even drastically different than your results tomorrow or in a few years. The notion of getting certain assessment results, which give us a label or put us into a category, needs to be fluid as we and our circumstances change. I think this should give some of the naysayers some confidence and hope because one of the big complaints against these assessments is that they are too discrete and define us for too long.

Your results are not permanent. They represent a snapshot based on imperfect questions, which you responded to while experiencing perhaps temporary circumstances or moods. If there are certain things in your personality that are out of alignment with who you really want to become, you're not stuck. You can actually work on skills and attributes and improve yourself. You can think about who you want to become and also how you want to act and start acting that way.

Allowing for change over time is a beautiful concept for us and for others. It allows us to grow and mature, to find ourselves and to make corrections. Going back to how someone was years ago could limit how we see them or how we allow them to express themselves. I invite you to keep this in mind as you get to work with different types of people over the years, especially the people who tend to rub you the wrong way or annoy you

Relationships vs. Work

Two end results we talk about in this Book are our relationships with others and productivity. I'm reminded of a fascinating conversation I had with a boss a few years ago where we talked about a leader's focus on one of these three, people, processes or systems, and product or results. I did an unscientific survey on Twitter where I asked which of the three was most important and was not surprised with the results.

Over 60% of the responses were that people were the most important. Product came in second and processes came in third. Contrast that, though, to the embarrassing statistic that somewhere around 75% of us are unhappy at work, even to the point of looking for other opportunities. As you learn about personalities in general and then personalities of people in your team, it's important to have the right objectives in mind. People are critically important. Losing the best people on your team could be devastating, even to the point of disintegrating the team.

I recognize that most of us need to have products or services, some deliverable, that justify our role on the team. The product you're working on can be the reason you are treated better, respected, and have better budgets. Great products combined with great sales and marketing create the opportunity to have a better environment for your people. Processes or systems are important for different reasons at different stages of an organisation. Sometimes they're critical, but we can put processes and products before people in a way that eventually will ruin what's called our human capital, the teams we've been building.

I can't argue which is most important for you because different organisations at different stages should prioritise differently;

however, I want to reiterate what Jim Collins said in his landmark book, Good to Great. We need to get the right people on the bus. And I'll add, keep the right people on the bus. This Book might help you identify who the right people could be and how to keep them on your bus. When you do that, you should see a measurable improvement in processes and products. Misunderstanding building and maintaining the right team and you might see serious problems with your processes and products.

QUICK RECAP

In this chapter, we lay a foundation for talking about personalities and how understanding different personalities and tendencies empower us. This understanding also helps us learn more about ourselves. We talked about working and communicating with others, as well as persuading and influencing. I shared some examples of working with different personalities from my own experience and talked about when understanding personalities can be really helpful.

We talked about preferences and tendencies and the concept of leading with. I shared thoughts from Vern, my friend, and then we talked about the sliding scale, as well as generalising. We talked about gaming the assessment, the impact of moods and circumstances, and critics and criticisms of assessments. We talked about assessments versus tests, allowing for change over time and people, processes, and products. In the next chapter, we'll dive into the Myers-Briggs since it is so common. When you're done with that chapter, you should have a really good idea of what it is and how it can help you understand personalities better. Let's go.

UNDERSTANDING THE MBTI

In this chapter, I want to focus on the Myers-Briggs Type Indicator, also known as the MBTI. I know some people don't like this assessment, but it has decades of prevalence in the corporate world. When I say corporate world, I mean even in government and noncommercial organisations.

Really, anywhere. And, the Myers-Briggs is a tool commonly used by career counsellors and therapists. The Myers-Briggs has become a standard in the personality assessment world and has influenced how we think about personalities. Let's jump in.

A KEY TO MBTI RESULTS: ROOT QUESTIONS

I've come to realise there's a very important, simple key to understanding Myers-Briggs results. In each survey, you have a list of questions. At the heart of each question is a root question. You aren't asked route questions, but understanding what they are can help you understand why you're asked each question and how you got the results you got. There's one root question for each of the four parts of the results. The first root question will help you determine if you are an I or an E.

The question is, are you outwardly or inwardly focused? You might guess an introvert is inwardly focused. As an example, I'm an introvert. When I'm in a meeting and need to process new, important information, I sometimes need a minute or two to quietly think about it. An extrovert might get nervous with the silence the introvert needs. Quiet time can be very uncomfortable for some people, but just realising it helps someone inwardly focused assess new information could be very helpful and remove discomfort. Realising extroverts like to think out loud can help you understand talking through it as an important part of their thinking. They're not rambling or stating the obvious, rather they are taking the information in.

Some extroverts need to go through this process, just as introverts need to go through their processes. The root question for the second position is how do you prefer to take in information? If you're sensing, then you prefer facts and details. If you're intuition, you prefer to take ideas and connect them so you can project beyond the facts. Someone who scores high on N, or intuition, also might like figurative or poetic descriptions. Knowing you're working with an N might lead you to use more stories, whereas if you're talking to an S, you'll need to incorporate more facts and details in your communication.

The root question for the third position is how do you prefer to make decisions? The thinking person tends to be more concerned about processes and systems than on people and their feelings, whereas the feeling person strives to please others. I once worked with a decisionmaker who was a strong F. There was a situation where someone had been let go from the company because of fraud. The terminated employee appealed to this strong F executive, and to everyone's surprise he actually got his job back.

Watching this play out in the workplace was fascinating. Even though the facts were clear and this person should not have been rehired, the F forgave the person and gave him another chance. I can imagine you're cringing as you listen to this example, but just understanding the boss was a feeling person helps us understand why he did it. The root question for the fourth position is how do you prefer to live your outer life? This is a weird question, isn't it? I don't think I've ever talked about my "outer" life in casual conversation. This might help explain the question. The judging person wants to settle their matters. They don't like to leave loose ends hanging.

The perceiving person might say, I'll take care of it when I get to it. That might be when they really have to make a decision, but until then, they're good to put it off. While the judging person prefers to have everything planned out, the perceiving person is fine to move forward without detailed plans. When you're trying to make sense of anyone's Myers-Briggs results, go back to these four root questions. Understanding these root questions can help you better understand MBTI results.

Introversion vs. Extroversion

Each of the four characters in your Myers-Briggs result represents your tendencies for certain questions. This first position in the results, which will be an I or an E, tries to answer the question, is your focus outward or inward? I represents introversion, while E represents extraversion. Of all the MBTI results, I'm guessing you are most familiar with introversion and extraversion. It's pretty common to talk about introverts being quiet, shy, nonparty types, and extraverts being loud and maybe without some social boundaries. Those are generalisations, Of course.

A few years ago, I remember the talk shifted from those stereotypes to how do you recharge? Introverts, for example, need to recharge by themselves, while extraverts need to recharge by being around others. Let's go into a few other characteristics you'll commonly find about introverts and extraverts. Introverts are typically described as reserved or private as opposed to extraverts who are described as talkative or outgoing. The introvert prefers a slower pace and likes time to think, whereas the extravert loves to be in a fast-paced environment. The introvert tends to think things through in their head while the extravert tends to work ideas out with others, which you might call thinking out loud.

The introvert would rather observe from a distance than be the centre of attention, whereas the extravert enjoys being the centre of attention. A quick note as we contrast each of the results from the Myers-Briggs assessment. There isn't necessarily a best or better result. We are all okay no matter what our results are. This isn't about getting a higher score or improving a personality over time. This is about understanding our and others tendencies and thinking about how relationships and communication are impacted by these tendencies.

Sensing vs. Intuition

The second position or character in the Myers-Briggs results will be an S or an N. S is for sensing, while N is for intuition. They didn't use I for intuition because I represent introverts. The main question at the root of these two results is how do you prefer to take in information? People who get an S for sensing tend to focus on reality and how they observe things to be right now. People who get an N for intuition are likely more able to imagine possibilities. They can imagine how things can be done. The sensing person likes facts and details and values this information when making decisions.

The intuitive person tends to look at the big picture, even without facts and details, and thinks about how things connect with one another. The sensing person prefers ideas that have practical applications, whereas the intuitive person enjoys ideas and concepts. A sensing person tends to describe things in a specific and literal way. They use facts, or what sound like facts, and details in their descriptions. The intuitive person describes things in a figurative or poetic way. If you think about the root question, how do you prefer to take in information, you can see this also impacts how you think about and communicate information.

Can you see how important understanding just a single aspect of you or someone else can help you better communicate with others? You may want a lot of data and details, but that might overwhelm an intuitive. Neither of you are wrong, but just knowing how you prefer to take in information can improve your relationship and communication.

Feeling vs. Thinking

The third position in the Myers-Briggs results will be either an F or a T, F for feeling and T for thinking. The question we're trying to answer is how do you prefer to make decisions? The feeling person makes decisions based on personal values and how actions affect others. They really think about the other person. On the other hand, the person scoring higher in thinking doesn't necessarily make decisions based on how the action would affect others. They tend to make decisions using logic and reasoning, which can feel very impersonal.

The feeling person values harmony and forgiveness, whereas the thinking person values justice and fairness. The feeling person likes to please others and point out the best in people. The thinking person enjoys finding the flaws in an argument. They're not as worried about pleasing others and making sure other people feel good as much as they want to make sure the argument is a good, solid argument. As you can imagine, a feeling person is typically described as someone who is warm and empathetic.

A thinking person might not be described as warm or empathetic. They're usually described as reasonable and levelheaded. Can you see that in some situations you'll want a feeling person, perhaps someone you can talk to and get empathy from, while other times you'll really want a thinking person. For example, if you need a lawyer for a very difficult legal situation.

Perceiving vs. Judging

The last of the four positions in your Myers-Briggs assessment will be a P or a J. P is for perceiving and J is for judging. The question we're trying to answer is kind of a weird one. How do you prefer to live your outer life? Outer life isn't a term I think I've ever used, but let's go through some of these characteristics and I think you'll understand what they're getting at. A perceiving person prefers to leave their options open while a judging person prefers to have their matters settled.

Have you ever worked with someone who before the meeting ends needs to have resolution to everything on the agenda? That person would probably tend to be a J for judging. A perceiving person sees rules and deadlines as flexible, whereas a judging person thinks rules and deadlines are more rigid and should be respected. If you score really high in judging, people who score high in perceiving are probably really annoying to you, especially on projects where there seems to be a lot at stake. A perceiving person likes to improve and make things up on the fly. They can go into a situation relying on their creativity and not worrying about having detailed plans.

A judging person would prefer to have detailed instructions. A perceiving person is spontaneous and enjoys surprises and new situations. The judging person likes to make plans and know every detail. The perceiving person seems to be a lot more laid back and ready to take on any challenge, whereas the judging person likes to prepare for every situation. If you're okay to hop in a car to take a road trip without a map and just drive, you're probably more of a perceiving person.

The person who has a full itinerary knows exactly where they're going, when they're going to get there, where they're going to stay, and what restaurants they'll eat at, that's the judging person.

SIMPLIFYING TYPES OF DESCRIPTIONS

A s with all assessments, the MBTI strives to simplify how we understand someone or their tendencies by using some type of label or class or categorization system. Using the four letters you see in the results is a simple way to help you understand someone's tendencies better, at least based on how they answered the questions. The funny thing about this attempt to simplify by categorising is that there are 16 possible results, which doesn't sound very simple.

The differences between one and another might be so small and so nuanced, it could be hard to tell the difference between them. Because Myers-Briggs is so common, there has been a lot of work done to help people understand what the results actually mean. People have come up with labels for each of the results. For example, the ENFJ is the teacher, while the ISTP is the craftsperson. A quick search online will show names for each of the 16 results. In the next few chapters, we'll talk about some of the MBTI results, walking through the combinations to help you get a better idea of how to decipher results. A quick search online will show names for each of the 16 results.

In the next few chapters, we'll talk about some of the MBTI results, walking through the combinations to help you get a better idea of how to decipher the results. Keep in mind, these labels are not necessarily ideal job titles, they are just labels people have created to help us understand what various combinations mean. Here's a quick overview. Supposedly the most common personality type is ISTJ, sometimes called the inspector. We'll talk more about the inspector in a few minutes. Again, supposedly, the least common personality type is INFJ, also known as the counsellor.

We'll go deeper into that in a few minutes. The more common MBTI results are the protector, the composer, the performer, and the provider. Isn't it interesting that the more common results are completely different personality types? Can you think of people you work with or in your personal life who might be a protector, a composer, a performer or a provider? The next most popular results are the crafter, the promoter, and the supervisor. Then you have the healer, the champion, and the teacher.

The least common results are the mastermind, the architect, the inventor, and the field marshal. Remember, these are summarised generalisations. Just because you or a colleague get certain MBTI results doesn't mean you are now the field marshal or the provider or whatever. Our personalities, preferences, and tendencies are more complex than one or two word labels. This information, the labels, and how common each of the results are is simply another piece of the vast puzzle of understanding ourselves and others.

UNDERSTANDING ISTJ (INSPECTOR)

I want to spend a few minutes going deeper into 4 of the 16 personality types. Doing this exercise four times should give you a thought process to help you build a profile you can use for any result. The first personality I want to talk about is the inspector, or ISTJ. Because the root questions are so important, I'll put them on the screen.

The first root question, the one that gives us the letter for the first of four characters, is are you outwardly or inwardly focused? ISTJ starts with an I, which means the inspector is introverted. The inspector tends to quietly think things through, be observant, and take time to contemplate things. How would knowing about these three preferences or tendencies help you communicate with or receive information from an ISTJ? If you're in a meeting with an inspector who doesn't talk much, are they mad at you? Are they disrespectful for not talking a lot? Or, could they just be thinking about the things that you're talking about?

It's easy to get offended when others don't talk to us, but understanding their preferences and tendencies can allow us to give them the space they need to think through their responses. The second root question is how do you prefer to take in information? The inspector, as a sensing person, wants facts and details. They want to understand the practical application of what you're talking about. They tend to describe things literally. The inspector is thoughtful about the information you give them. If I were trying to persuade an ISTJ, I would make sure I had good, solid facts and lots of details ready.

The third root question is how do you prefer to make decisions? The inspector is a T, which means thinking instead of F for feeling. This means that, with regard to making decisions, the inspector tends to be impersonal and logical, valuing justice and fairness. They seek flaws in arguments and they're typically described as being level headed. The fourth root question is how do you prefer to live your outer life? The ISTJ is a judging person, which means they like to have their matters settled. They like rules and deadlines. They like detailed instructions and they like to have and make plans.

According to what I've read, the inspector is the most common personality type in the United States. Can you see how understanding the characteristics of the inspector can help you understand how and what you would communicate to them and why they communicate a certain way with you? You wouldn't want to go into a meeting with just stories and anecdotes, you need facts and details.

Try to appeal to the inspector's sense of justice and fairness by explaining processes and rules, appeal to their introverted nature by allowing them time to contemplate. Giving the inspector a deadline might appeal to the way they think.

UNDERSTANDING ISFJ (PROTECTOR)

The next most common personality type is the ISFJ, sometimes called the protector. As we go through this exercise, I want you to think about how you might do something similar for people you know who aren't one of these four types we're going to dig into. This process should help you understand how you can give them information in the best way. This information can help you persuade others to think or act a certain way.

The protector has three of the same characteristics as the last personality type we talked about, namely introvert, sensing, and judging. The only difference between the inspector and the protector is the third position, which is F for feeling instead of T for thinking. The root question for feeling or thinking is how do you prefer to make decisions? The feeling person cares about a person's feelings and how information, decisions, and actions will affect others. They like making decisions based on harmony and relationships. The feeling person likes to please others.

The protector values facts and details. They like to have a clear picture of what's going on. They like to think through all the details. But when it comes down to making decisions, they are definitely considerate of people's feelings and how they might be perceived. Does knowing that the protector prefers to make decisions with these characteristics help you know how to better approach or communicate with an ISFJ? You can see how this knowledge can be really powerful.

UNDERSTANDING ESFJ (PROVIDER)

T he third most common personality type is the ESFJ, also known as the provider. You can see with the S that they're sensing, which means they like facts and details. The J says they are judging people, which means they like to have a conclusion to their issues and appreciate deadlines. The provider appreciates plans and doesn't like surprises. The F shows they are feeling people who actually care about other people's feelings. The main difference here is switching from introvert to extrovert.

Because the provider is an extravert, they tend to be more talkative and outgoing. They like to be in fast-paced situations. They tend to think out loud and be the centre of attention. How does knowing someone is extraverted help you deal with that person? Being extraverted doesn't mean they're better or worse, right or wrong, we're just using this information to have better relationships and better communication. If you're working with a provider, maybe you let them be the spokesperson for your team.

They might want and appreciate this much more than an introvert would. When communicating with a provider, remember, they like data, facts, and details. They care about your feelings and like to come to a conclusion with their projects, all characteristics they share with a protector, they might just be more loud and vocal.

UNDERSTANDING INFJ (COUNSELLOR)

In this final example, we'll look at the INFJ, also known as the counsellor. Supposedly this is the least common personality type in the United States. The root question we're answering that impacts the second letter is how do you prefer to take in information? The results are either S for sensing or N for intuition. In the case of the counsellor, it is N for intuition. People who are N think about how things could be. They see the big picture and the connections that are made between things. They like ideas and concepts.

I mean they're introverted. The counsellor will be thoughtful, they'll see the big picture, maybe things that are on or beyond the horizon. They'll want their matters settled and they'll appreciate rules and deadlines. Sounds like a great person to have on most teams. Now that we've gone through four examples, I'd like you to write down the names of three to five people, whether they are people you work with or have personal relationships with. Guess what their Myers-Briggs assessment results might be and then list characteristics for each person based on each of the four letters.

As you do this, think about your experiences with them. How do they tend to act and communicate? You might be able to identify certain traits, tendencies or preferences that make a lot more sense with this information and through the lens of the Myers-Briggs assessment. Thinking through this can help you identify times where you communicated well with them or perhaps didn't communicate well at all.

This might seem like a tedious exercise, but we're talking about your career, relationships, and communication. When you strive to understand yourself and others, you are closer to better relationships and richer communication. This investment is definitely worth your attention.

FORGIVENESS, FLEXIBILITY, AND JOB FIT

Humans are exceptionally complex. Labelling and stereotyping into nice, precise little buckets or boxes is convenient, but it can do us and others a great disservice. These assessments attempt to help us understand ourselves and others based on preferences and tendencies, but preferences and tendencies are not absolutes. Results can be used to predict, but they won't be 100% accurate all the time.

When someone acts contrary to what their assessment results say they would, that's okay. Perhaps they're making conscious decisions to do something intentional in a way that is different, even difficult for them. Being intentional makes actions and reactions more special. Knowledge and assumptions about personalities can be abused. You could look at someone and say you're an introvert, no wonder you act like that, or you're an introvert, you should act differently. Please don't use this information to manipulate or unfairly stereotype others.

We need to make sure we forgive people for shortcomings in how they act or communicate. We're all human, right? Let people be human. Let others act within their strengths while still having weaknesses. Forgiving people puts us in a different mindset and might even help us learn how to forgive ourselves for our shortcomings. The Myers-Briggs Type Indicator gives us information, but we need to allow for flexibility. Don't expect everyone to always act the way they should based on assessment results. Maybe those results were off because of when they took the test or circumstances that influence their answers.

Many times, Myers-Briggs results are used to determine job fit or how well someone might fit into a team. These assessments can have a real significant impact on your future. Take them seriously if they're used in your organisation or if they are important to your boss. A key takeaway from this Book is to allow for forgiveness and flexibility when working and communicating with others.

WHAT THIS MEANS

The Myers-Briggs Type Indicator is merely a tool. It's time tested, having been used for decades around the world. It has become a popular lens through which we try to understand what motivates others, who they are, and what makes them tick. It's also a tool that has plenty of controversy. It's not perfect. Maybe it's a little too complex. Maybe it's a little too simple. There are other tools that claim to be more effective than the Myers-Briggs. I want you to look at it for what it is, simply a tool. It gives us data or information by which we can make decisions and judgments.

The data or information can be flawed, swayed by feelings or circumstances. Even so, we can use this information along with other information we have to get a better understanding of people. Keep in mind, the goal is to understand ourselves and others, and we should use any tool that can help with that. Feel free to learn more about the pros and cons of MBTI and then consider those things as you use the results. If nothing else, please think about the I and the E, the S and the N, the F and the T and the P and the J.

Think about what each of those letters mean and how they impact your understanding of others. The more you dig into this, the more you'll see important characteristics and personality traits in others and in yourself. Like I said earlier, knowledge of human nature isn't just a power, it's a superpower

QUICK RECAP

In this chapter, we explored the Myers-Briggs Type Indicator to help us understand what the MBTI assesses and what the results mean. We talked about the root questions and then differentiated between introversion and extraversion, sensing and intuition, feeling and thinking, and perceiving and judging. We went into 4 of 16 personality types to better understand what those types meant and better understand what each letter means. We talked about the idea of flexibility with labels and categories, and now here we are wrapping up this chapter.

In the next chapter, we're going to talk about a different assessment tool, the DiSC assessment. This is another common tool we see organisations use to help us understand ourselves and one another. Let's get started.

UNDERSTANDING DISC

The Myers-Briggs isn't the only personality tool to help people understand themselves and one another. There are others I've come across that, in certain circles, have gained traction. The colour code is probably the first one I heard of with people saying that person is so red or that person is blue. I wasn't sure what red meat, but I correctly assumed it had to do with having a strong personality. There are other colours in various variations of this model, including white, green, gold, pink, etc., but usually people talk about four main colours.

As a newly married husband, I learned about a book called Personality Plus, which has four personality types: phlegmatic, sanguine, melancholy, and choleric. If that sounds familiar, I'm guessing you have heard of the four temperaments of Greek origin from over a couple thousand years ago. Reading this book as newlyweds helped us have common language as we learned about ourselves and one another.

Another book that caught my attention through my wife is It's Just my Nature by Carol Tuttle. This model has, get this, four categories to help describe personalities, which are 1, 2, 3, and 4. It's a fascinating approach that fills in some gaps the other tools have. In this chapter, I want to talk about the DiSC personality assessment. DiSC is the other assessment tool that has seen a lot of traction in the professional or corporate world. Let's dive in to understand the what and why of the DiSC assessment tool.

DISC OVERVIEW

Because no one owns DiSC, there are multiple versions that are based on the DiSC methodology. This means there are a bunch of different ways DiSC can be administered and interpreted. With that in mind, I'll try to stay as general as I can, respecting nuances from different organisations. Each of the four letters in DiSC stand for something. D stands for dominance. I stand for influence. S stands for steadiness. C stands for conscientious. Your DiSC results might be something like D or D/S.

It could even be D/S/C. Mirroring what I've said before and consistent with similar tools, you lead with one and are a mix of the others. If your primary style is D for dominance, you want to win. If you think a dominant person is bossy, you might be right, but dig deeper to understand what the dominant person is about, what drives them. They need to win. They work to create an environment and team so they can win. Sometimes, though, the dominant person seems like they don't care about others because they are so focused on winning. The style is influenced.

Think of the person who strives to bring people together to influence and persuade others. This might be the person who says come on team, let's do this. They might be known for their high energy, excitement, and enthusiasm. On the other hand, they might be known for being unorganised and maybe a little too light on facts and details. The S, or steadiness style, indicates you likely work to get the job done and reduce contention in your team. You want harmony, people working together and enjoying the team. You like rules, roles, and order.

You might be the one to say, come on, can't we all just get along? The conscientious person likes to learn and share what they've learned. They appreciate quality and accuracy. They might be seen as a perfectionist, which can be annoying in some situations, but really valuable in others. Actually, any of these traits can feel annoying in some situations, but valuable in others, and that's one of the recurring themes in this Book. There is no right or wrong way to be. Please accept and internalise this for yourself and for others.

The goal here is not to become the same, rather to gain understanding of ourselves and others and learn how these traits and characteristics can help improve working relationships and communication with others.

OBSERVABLE BEHAVIOURS

One of the things I really like about the DiSC assessment is that it is basing results on your observable behaviour and observable emotions. This is an important distinction because the Myers-Briggs questions are more about what you think you would do while DiSC is more about things you have done. Observable behaviour means the heart of each question is when you had this situation before, how did you react?

While the Myers-Briggs questions get at preferences and tendencies, which some say are internal, the DiSC questions get at observable behaviours, which they say are external. I really do like this distinction. I find it hard to answer some of the Myers-Briggs questions because I think, well, under ideal circumstances, I would do this thing or I think someone like me should answer this way. It's like I'm constantly reassessing or second guessing my internal, my preferences and tendencies. With the DiSC, I can answer questions thinking how did I actually handle certain scenarios? That goes beyond the ideal answer.

I really like the idea of asking how I've reacted or thought. I think it's easier to answer these questions more accurately. This is important because the focus is on what we have done and what we think we would do based on past behaviour. You've probably heard some variation of this phrase, past behaviour is a great indicator of future behaviour. Combine this different kind of questioning with a scaling system of responses instead of just choosing one or two options, and you have assessment questions that might help you get more precise results.

DEBRIEF BEHAVIOURS

As with any similar assessment or test result, you should figure out how to debrief your results. DiSC administrators are trained to debrief results with you so you can really understand at a more granular level what the results mean. Even though you might be a D/S, or whatever, your DiSC results can be pages and pages long. Talking to a trained DiSC administrator can really help you understand your results. I'm a big fan of debriefing.

I talk about it in some of my other Books as a step to help ensure you maximise learning and understanding. In this specific example, I invite you to have a qualified DiSC administrator debrief your results with you. In other situations, or if you can't find a DiSC administrator, I invite you to debrief with someone else or even just by yourself. To debrief by yourself, set aside time without distractions to really ponder the information you have. Think about your opportunities or what the information means. What impact could this have on your career, your relationships, your communication, and your future?

What could you learn about yourself that might increase job satisfaction or help you manage expectations you have about yourself? I recommend journaling your thoughts and ideas, epiphanies, and action items. This could be in a physical journal, a book you actually write in, or it could be in a series of emails you write to yourself or a document on the cloud, which is where I tend to record thoughts like these. There's power in journaling, and this is something worth your time. The questions I asked just a few seconds ago could be answered and revisited over time. The idea is to really get to know yourself.

DiSC results are complex enough that you should spend time pondering and debriefing, but really, any personality assessment results you get should be debriefed. Whether you talk to a close friend who will be honest with you to ask about the validity of your results or you spend a lot of time journaling your thoughts, I encourage you to have a thorough debrief.

COMPLEMENTARY
PEOPLE

One of the benefits we should get from understanding personalities, tendencies, preferences, types, and styles is that we can understand who we would best work with. I know someone who is a dominant, a strong D, which means they are direct, firm, strong-willed, and forceful. They tend to work great with others unless there are other Ds, or dominants. The Ds seem to have a hard time figuring out who the main dominant is.

I'm not saying it can't be done, but from what I've seen, some dominants will have to kind of relinquish control and power to another or else there will be a lot of arguing and eventual factions. When you pair a dominant with an S, which, remember, S stands for steadiness, you get kind of a power partnership. The steady partner has complementary characteristics that may allow them to overlook what others might see as annoying or overbearing in the dominant. And the dominant can really appreciate and work with the steady person in a way that perhaps would annoy others. Imagine a team with all dominants or all steady.

You would miss out on diversity of thoughts and skills. Having different styles work together and optimally complement one another can be extremely powerful. I'm not saying you can't have people with non complementary styles on a team. Of course you can, and Of course you can create a great team with those people. I'm just suggesting that you consider personality types or styles as you build or rebuild teams.

Thinking about personality types or styles that complement one another can help you build powerful teams. If you think about it, creating winning teams is why many organisations and recruiters want you to do personality assessments.

COMPLEMENTARY STYLES

Okay, so, we know your DiSC results are called a behavioural style. Your primary style might be a D or I or S or C. Expect a secondary style that complements your primary style. This is directly in line with what we've talked about with sliding scales and not being absolute. Remember, DiSC results number in the thousands, so there's definitely a lot of sliding. Look at what the secondary and tertiary styles are and how strong those styles are.

An idea behind all of these assessments is that we can get a better understanding of who we are and why we think and do things the way we do. We also need to understand those things about people we work with, our customers, our leaders, even people we have personal relationships with. Considering complementary styles will help us understand or even just think about some of these nuances that vary from the primary style. If you talk to someone who is an I and they act differently than you expect, it could be because they're secondary style is coming out. This very idea is basically a theme of the Book.

Make sure you respect the sliding scale and recognize that a dominant style or assessment result is not the only style or result. Just having this perspective can help explain unexpected behaviour. Of course, this goes hand in hand with the role circumstances play. As I mentioned earlier, allow for flexibility when comparing behaviours and results.

BEHAVIOURAL STRENGTHS AND SOFT SKILLS

If you have seen any of my other Books or the titles of my Books, you'll know I'm passionate about soft skills. I've seen the impact soft skills have on my own career when hiring others, when intense situations, in helping preserve important relationships, when making sales, and more. In my Book, Leading with Emotional Intelligence, I talk about soft skills a lot.

Every single one of the five pillars of emotional intelligence has everything to do with soft skills. They're so important that the fifth pillar, social skills, is even sometimes called soft skills. Soft skills help us communicate better, understand others, and have richer and more appropriate relationships. Soft skills are an excellent complement to hard skills. Imagine being great at whatever technical proficiencies you need to have and being able to communicate in an effective way with others, which is what soft skills help with. I believe soft skills, like any skill, can be learned and improved on.

To get better at any soft skill, you should have an awareness of the skill, perhaps learn tactics and techniques, and regularly practise those skills. Sometimes you'll see quick improvement, other times you'll feel like you're working on them for years and not seeing much progress. The DiSC assessment tells you what your behavioural strengths are. If you look at those strengths, you should draw correlations to soft skills. Some of those soft skills will be great in some situations. For example, listening might be one of your prominent skills if you're an S, while taking commands might be a prominent skill if you are a D. Thinking about your DiSC results through this lens, I invite you to think about two ideas.

The first is to think about what soft skills you inherently have or practice based on your assessment results. If you're an S, you are probably a naturally good listener. What if you spent time working on listening skills with best practice techniques and tactics? What if you really become disciplined in your natural strength and get further training? I encourage you to get better at what comes natural to you. You might be good or great at it. What if you worked on becoming excellent at it? The second idea is to think about what you are not naturally good at, but should be. What soft skills could help you be more effective in your role? If you are a D and are naturally good at problem solving, what soft skills could make you a more effective communicator?

I've worked with dominant people who were excellent at problem solving, but not very good at reading the room or understanding others. Dominants want to get a problem solved very quickly, and sometimes they do that in a way that feels harsh to others. What if you, as a D, worked on empathy and persuasion? You could marry your natural strength of problem solving with a skill that helps you communicate more effectively. Can you imagine how powerful those two skills could be together? Here's my twofold invitation.

Work on the skills that come naturally to you with more discipline and training and figure out what soft skills complement those skills associated with your disk results and make a plan to improve those. One of my hopes for you is continual growth, especially in soft skills. These two tactics could lead to some serious personal growth.

ASSESSMENT RESULTS AND YOUR BRAND

A s we wrap up these two chapters where we explored the Myers-Briggs and the DiSC assessments, I want to talk about one of my favourite topics, personal branding. I have a Book on personal branding which includes a bunch of tactics you can use to create and reinforce the right brand for you. Regarding these assessments, I want to share an opportunity and a cautionary warning. The opportunity is to take things you've learned and use words, phrases, and ideas to craft your branding statements. There might be things you've learned from your experience with the MBTI and the DiSC assessment that you never really thought about.

I know I've had characteristics I didn't put much thought into until I saw them in my results. Once you have this information, you can start to talk about it more. This includes in interviews, networking situations, on resumes, and your LinkedIn profile, etc. Wherever you put branding statements, you can put some of this information. I'm not saying that you have to, but you can. I want you to be intentional and strategic about what you include in your branding statements, which I talk about in my Personal Branding Book. Here are some examples. I work best when I have lots of projects to work on. I excel at leading others and I work well in stressful environments.

I am not necessarily a good team leader, but I thrive when I have consistent work to do and the right resources. You can see I'm using insights from assessment results to talk up strengths or even answer interview questions like what is one of your greatest weaknesses. My cautionary warning is just as important, beware of assumptions and stereotypes that come with labels and generalisations, even from assessment results. When people find out you're an INFJ or a C/S, they might make all kinds of wrong assumptions about you. One of the great things about these assessment results is that we can easily categorise and group people.

One of the worst things about these assessment results is that we can easily, too easily, categorise and group people. When people learn you are an introvert, they might stereotype you with introvert attributes. They might be correct or they could be way off. After speaking on stage, I've had people come up and say, huh, you were a programmer? I didn't know programmers could be public speakers. This was an assumed attribute based on a stereotype that people put on me that was clearly wrong. The same thing can happen to you. One of my main points in my Personal Branding Book is that people already have assumptions about you. Many times they are wrong and many times they are not what you want them to be.

I want you to be intentional about your brand. If you aren't, you'll still have a brand, it will just be the wrong brand. So, learn about your personality results and make sure you create some branding statements to help break out of stereotypes. For example, I know I'm an introvert, but I actually thrive in certain social situations. You can put me in front of customers, prospects, and executives and I can make a very compelling and persuasive presentation. That's not to say that introverts can't do that, but a lot of people think introverts will freeze in front of people. This is a simple example of overcoming stereotypes to help define and refine your personal brand. Please read my Personal branding Book and intentionally work on your brand.

QUICK RECAP

In this chapter, we focused on the DiSC assessment. We talked about what the DiSC assessment is and how it helps you understand personality styles. We talked about how you can understand ideas, like how tasks are approached and at what speed people work. We talked about the importance of debriefing as a part of the process of understanding your DiSC results.

We talked about complementary styles and how your behavioural strengths are your soft skills. In the next chapter, we'll tie a lot of these ideas together and talk about understanding personalities on our quest for better relationships and more effective communication.

BETTER RELATIONSHIPS AND COMMUNICATION

In this Book, we've talked about two common tools to help us understand why people are the way they are. These tools aren't flawless, but they're common enough that you'll likely experience them at work. They do a decent job of helping us unravel the complexities of human nature. I want you to understand yourself, your own tendencies and preferences, as much as I want you to understand others.

Just understanding yourself can help with your relationships and communication. While these tools are neat and can be helpful, remember why we are using them, to improve relationships and communication. Let's talk more about that in this chapter.

UNDERSTANDING YOURSELF

L eading with Emotional Intelligence is one of my favourite and most important Books I've done on Amazon. In that Book, I talk about the five pillars of emotional intelligence. The first is self-awareness. I'd say self-awareness is one of the most important life skills. Greater self-awareness can lead to a healthier perspective of who you are, where you're at, and perhaps a path you can get on for improved happiness, satisfaction, and fulfilment.

Honest self-awareness can also lead to self-confidence. I hear a lot of self-defeating talk from technologists who always feel behind in their tech skills. Technologists need to constantly learn, which might be why I hear the phrase imposter syndrome so often. When we have self-awareness, we are prepared to have better, more appropriate, more effective self-regulation, which is the third pillar of emotional intelligence. Self-regulation helps us manage things like imposter syndrome, feelings of being overwhelmed, or when we're in a meeting and we don't understand what's going on.

The person who understands himself can be in a stressful situation, and instead of blowing up and getting out of control, practice techniques to calm down, assess the situation, remove unnecessary emotion and negative self-talk, and act professionally. I know it can be hard to unpack who you are and honestly look at your strengths and weaknesses.

Hopefully by now, you see I'm not talking about doing a deep assessment on your weaknesses, rather your tendencies and preferences. You aren't better or worse than others and you aren't right or wrong, you are who you are. Knowing that and accepting that can help improve your communication and relationships.

UNDERSTANDING OTHERS

When you understand your preferences and tendencies regarding how you want to receive information, you understand why you might share information with others in a way that makes sense to you, but might not consider how they want to receive information. The fourth pillar of emotional intelligence is sometimes called empathy, sometimes called awareness of others. I think awareness of others empowers us to have more and more appropriate empathy.

Awareness of others means we hear others, we see them, and we seek to understand them. I've had plenty of personal and professional relationships where I've not understood others, their intentions, and how they prefer to give or receive information, and that has had a profound impact on my relationships. I'm not saying that understanding others means you will have better relationships with everyone you meet. There are going to be people you don't agree with, don't like, and don't want to be around. That's fine. But understanding others, their preferences, and tendencies could help you better understand why you don't like them or why you aren't communicating effectively with them.

This awareness can help you make improvements or make a

mature decision on how to proceed with the relationship. At work, where we sometimes don't have the luxury of moving away from certain people or relationships, understanding others can help you get work done better and in a more enjoyable way, not because you are changing other people, rather because you learn why they do and think and communicate the way they do. Understanding others can help remove bad emotions and petty likes and dislikes from your personal and professional relationships.

Earlier in this Book, I talked about a superpower. Learning how to persuade and influence others can be your superpower. An important component of this superpower is understanding who you want to persuade and influence.

ALLOWING FOR FLEXIBILITY AND SCALABILITY

Two of my favourite words with software and products are flexibility and scalability, or really personal growth. I loved the idea of creating flexible code, meaning it could be used in various scenarios, even scenarios we hadn't thought about. I also loved creating code that would scale, products that could grow as needed because they were designed for growth. This made the code or the final output adaptable to changes. I found one of the most constant changes in this world is people.

People are constantly growing, learning, facing experiences and challenges, coming into good fortune or bad fortune, and coming to terms with themselves all the time. I've already talked about allowing for flexibility with assessment results, recognizing a margin of error or results that were impacted by mood or other circumstances. I want to emphasise that people change. There are experiences we have in life that create great change, such as job loss, death of a loved one or another tragedy like a car accident. These experiences can change the way we think about society and our place in society.

Other changes might come from promotions or lack of

promotions. When I was in high school I had a pretty solid view of myself; I had high self-confidence and a very optimistic outlook on my future. Since then, I've had a number of experiences that were not aligned with my optimistic outlook. I've experienced failures and setbacks that have impacted my perspective. I continued to be optimistic, but there were times when I was ready to give up and change careers or make other significant changes in my life. Some of the changes we experience are subtle and happen over long periods of time.

They might come from wins or losses we have. They can impact how we think, how we open or close ourselves to relationships, and how we communicate with others. Someone you worked with 10 years ago might be a completely different person than who they are today. You might be a completely different person than who you were 10 years ago. I invite you to allow for change and allow how you perceive yourself and others to change.

BEST ROLES FOR PERSONALITIES

O ne of the reasons companies, recruiters, and career counsellors like personality assessments is because it gives them data they can use to align people and their personalities with roles. I haven't always agreed with the results I've gotten from career counsellors, especially when I was in high school. They seemed to be reaching for weird job titles. I'm sure it was backed up by lots of data, but I already thought I knew what I wanted to do for a living, and none of their results matched that.

Still, though, if you're not happy with your role, perhaps it makes sense to look at what the results tell you. Take some assessments, maybe multiple times, to figure out what you might average out to and then do research on best careers for those results. Knowing what I know now, my questions would have been what do these results have in common and what is it about these jobs or roles that I'm supposed to be a fit for? For example, a quick online search shows the best jobs for an ISTJ includes accountant and programmer.

Now that you understand what an I and S and T and J mean, that makes sense, doesn't it? I'm not saying you will only find success in a job that is aligned with your assessment results. I'm sure there are people who are not ISTJs that would do well at the jobs listed for ISTJs, but perhaps those are the jobs where you'll find the most job satisfaction and fulfilment. Those jobs might be well aligned with your preferences and tendencies. Use assessment results as data points as you learn more about yourself. Just remember, these are but a few of many data points.

When I was in my university's computer program, I was surprised that anyone would think being in liberal arts, like humanities or theatre, could be a good career choice. I remember arrogantly thinking that everyone should study computers. Doesn't that sound horrible? I'm sad to admit, that is how I thought back then. I eventually realised a successful organisation can benefit from all kinds of people. You need the persistent salesperson, You need the introverted and shy developer.

You need an accountant who could spend hours on spreadsheets. You need the creative minds for writing better copy and creating beautiful designs and graphics. My thinking finally aligned with the idea that there is no right or wrong personality. No one is better or worse. All personalities and skills can add value somewhere, and they are all necessary.

TWO KEYS TO YOUR SUCCESS

There is a lot of information in this Book. My intention isn't to make you a Myers-Briggs or DISC expert, rather I want to give you enough information so you could start to make sense of the personalities around you. There are two things I think that are key to your success with this knowledge. First, understand what your preferences are. How do you prefer to receive information, how do you prefer to make decisions, and other questions we've talked about in this Book.

Instead of wishing you were someone else or comparing yourself to others, just own what your preferences are. You shouldn't be ashamed of or embarrassed about your preferences or personality type or style. When you understand your preferences, you can recognize your strengths and know what situations you would excel in. You can also recognize your weaknesses and help people understand what a great or poor match is for you. With this honest assessment and understanding, you can determine the skills you should focus on.

If you have weaknesses in certain areas you know you should work on, focus on those. The second key is to appropriately communicate this information with others. It usually doesn't do you any good to hide your strengths, preferences, and tendencies from others. As you communicate your preferences, you increase the chances to have better relationships and more effective communication. When a team communicates personality types, preferences, and tendencies, we can become aware of who will excel in which situations and perhaps who shouldn't do certain things like present in front of executives.

You can better ensure each person contributes with their greatest abilities and strengths and even identify who should get specialised training. I'm not saying people shouldn't grow into certain tasks or roles, but knowing your preferences and tendencies could help you know when you might need to team up with someone who has strengths that complement your personality. Appropriately communicating this information can help your team be more effective.

PERSONALITIES
AND WORKING
WITH OTHERS

As you learn to understand yourself and others with an allowance for forgiveness and flexibility, you are putting yourself in a better position of enhanced work relationships. Instead of going to work and dreading the people you work with, maybe because you don't understand them or they don't understand you, you can work around differences. You can be a more effective teammate and appreciate others for what they bring to the team. Instead of feeling annoyed or even jealous of how others work, you can appreciate differences and diversity in your teams.

You see that effective teams need different strengths, and you can value or even express appreciation for what everyone brings. As everyone on your team appreciates one another's personalities, preferences, and tendencies, your team gets to a point where personality quirks don't matter. You can focus more on the task at hand and on delivering better products and services for your customers. Can you imagine how great that team would be? You should see an increase in job satisfaction, which is something HR is usually acutely concerned about, as well as retention and productivity.

This work environment becomes fun, it is a team you want to be a part of, you find yourself giving your best because you know your work is seen and valued and you know your teammates are competent and high contributors. This is my vision, creating better work environments because we have less friction with people and different personalities. This doesn't happen when we ignore different behaviour, rather because we increase our understanding of personalities and human nature.

PERSONALITIES AND COMMUNICATION WITH OTHERS

Increased understanding of personalities, preferences, and tendencies should also lead to improvements in your communication. When you're in a meeting or presentation, listen for clues indicating personality characteristics of people who are trying to make a point or sell you on an idea. Do they use details and data or do they stick to stories and anecdotes?

If you want facts and details and they want stories and anecdotes, there could be a problem. This can be frustrating. Understanding how you prefer to receive information and how others prefer to receive information can have a profound influence on your ability to communicate. When you know what the people you need to effectively communicate with want, even need, details and facts, you can better cater your communication for them.

Can you imagine how effective your communication can be with this one bit of knowledge? You're better prepared to think about how others prefer to receive information and deliver exactly what might influence and impact them. I've been in presentations where the presenter didn't do that. They were cut short by an executive who said something to the effect of getting to the point.

The point wasn't a feel good story, which is what the presenter was inspired by, rather it was the facts or details the executive wanted to hear. You can avoid this embarrassing situation with the knowledge and understanding from this Book.

Here are examples of how understanding personalities might influence your communication. When talking to an introvert in a group, don't draw attention to them as you might when talking to an extrovert. When talking to a sensing person, use facts and details. When talking to a thinking person, focus on logical arguments. When talking to a judging person, focus on what you want them to do to bring an issue to a close. Why? Because the judging person values getting things done and crossed off their list.

As a professional presenter, I've heard I need to focus on the audience hundreds of times. This is communication 101. As you focus on your audience, which might be a customer or your teammates, focus on their tendencies and preferences. This can greatly enhance your communication effectiveness.

PERSONALITIES AND INFLUENCING OTHERS

The third thing I want to talk about is completely intertwined with better relationships and better communication. We have opportunities to influence others many times a day. We influence them to give us more resources or time. Maybe we need more information or introductions to others. Perhaps we need them to buy in or sign off. As we improve our relationships, we put ourselves in a position to influence others.

As we learn how to more effectively communicate with others, we're in a better position to influence others. I've known people who are masters of influence. I'm not sure how much training they've had or if this just comes naturally to them, but I've seen them influence others, and it's mesmerising. I'm not talking about influencing in a bad way, but effective influencers seem to get their way a lot. They have thought through what they want, understand why it's best for everyone, and then work on communicating that to others.

Influencing others can have a great impact on your career. You might find more success with your projects and products, you might find it's easier to get customers to use your tools the way they should, prospects to buy your stuff or executives to support your initiatives.

This comes more naturally when you understand the personalities, preferences, and tendencies of your customers, prospects, and executives, when you understand how they prefer to receive information and how they make decisions, when you understand how you tend to communicate and what you should adjust to more effectively communicate with and persuade them. What an amazing opportunity you have to impact your career as you learn how to influence others for everyone's benefit.

YOUR LIFELONG
JOURNEY

I invite you to think about these things for the rest of your life. Seriously. As long as you have others in your life with opportunities for personal and professional relationships and the need to have effective communication, you should think about these things. I'm sure you won't become an expert in this knowledge or application of this knowledge by the end of this Book; however, as you practise better relationships and communication based on knowing more about human nature, you should be able to make marginal and even noticeable improvements.

Having this as a part of your lifelong journey means sometimes you will do well and feel like you're making progress and other times you'll feel like you're failing. When you've had bad relationship experiences or bad communication, take it as a learning experience. Maybe you were just wrong or you chose a wrong communication tactic; learn from that and strive to improve later.

Don't let a mistake weigh you down or define you as bad at relationships or communication. Maybe you take a few months or a year to focus on a certain aspect of communication or relationships and get really good at that aspect. Give yourself time to get better at these things. Don't focus on the times you fail, rather, celebrate when you do something exceptionally well, like when you go outside of your preferences and tendencies to persuade someone who has different preferences and tendencies.

This, by the way, is not a lack of authenticity, rather it is understanding others and how to most effectively communicate with them. These winds add up over time. They'll become a part of your muscle memory. You'll build important, even critical skills, that will help you in ways you may not have thought possible. This doesn't happen overnight.

CONCLUSION

In this chapter, we talked about various ideas to bring these concepts of personalities, relationships, and communication together. We talked about understanding yourself and others and how those tie into emotional intelligence. We talked about flexibility and scaling, roles based on personalities, two keys to your success, working with others, communicating with others, influencing others, and how this is a lifelong journey.

I feel strongly that this knowledge can really help every aspect of your life professionally and personally, as well as your relationship with yourself. Please work on this every day for the rest of your life. I wish you well as your relationships improve and your communication becomes more effective.

www.ingramcontent.com/pod-product-compliance
Lightning Source LLC
Chambersburg PA
CBHW071138220526
45467CB00015B/1410